ALL ABC

DEVILS

by

Moses Hull
(1835-1907)

- Ancient Grimoires -
Series
(a part of Templum Dianae Media)

Work edited by "Templum Dianae Media."
Illustrations and cover by "Templum Dianae Media"
Layout and formatting by "Templum Dianae Media"
back page and curated introduction by "Templum Dianae Media"

2023 - All Rights Reserved

Before you continue reading, the author and publisher explicitly ask that you read and understand the legal notes to clarify some basic aspects of the relationship between the parties.

Legal note:

this book is subject to exclusive copyright; reading it is intended for personal use only. It should also be noted that it is absolutely not permitted to modify or use any of the sections of this book, either for free or for a fee; it is absolutely not permitted to use, quote or paraphrase any section or sections of this book or its contents without the written and signed consent of the author and/or publisher.

Legal notice about the non-liability of the author and publisher:

The author and publisher affirm and reiterate that all the information contained in this work, taken individually or in its entirety, depending on the sensibilities of the individual reader or reader, may have a didactic-educational purpose or that of mere pastime.

The author and publisher of this volume, while reminding all readers that no warranty of any kind is explicitly or implicitly given, affirm and reiterate that all the information contained in this work, being derived from critical reading of various sources, possesses the highest degree of accuracy, reliability, topicality and completeness in relation to their ability to research, synthesize, process and organize the information.

Readers are aware that the author is in no way obligated to provide any kind of legal, financial, medical, or professional assistance or advice, and indeed recommends that they, before attempting any of the techniques or actions set forth in this book, contact a professional legally licensed to practice, as per current legislation.

By reading this introduction, each reader agrees, explicitly or implicitly, that in no event shall the author and/or publisher be liable for any loss, direct or indirect, resulting from the use of the information contained in this book, including but not limited to errors, omissions, or inaccuracies.

www.templumdianae.co

Ancient Grimoire Series

Ancient Grimoire Series, is a part of publishing Project "Templum Dianae".

Templum Dianae has been involved in the creation and dissemination of material of philosophical and esoteric interest for more than 10 years, with the aim of helping aspiring initiates, or work brothers to find quality educational material.

For this, the "Ancient Grimoires" rib, is in charge of selecting the best reprints of the past, re-adapting them for new technologies and making them available again for printing to the public, and providing new life and new luster to the great works, and great initiates of the past.

For this reason, the book you are holding in your hands represents not only an important piece of history of our past, but one of the cornerstones of esotericism, which you absolutely must know in order to progress on your path!

Teaching Materials included

Scan this code to get
your Video Course included in the book, an introduction to the world
of the occult and the paranormal

Or follow this link:

https://templumdianae.co/the-witchy-course/

This Material will give you access to Exclusive training materials to improve in your path !

PREFACE.

As a general thing I do not intend to write anything that needs an apology. As for the *matter* of this book, I am sure no apology is needed. The world needs it. Devils and hob-goblins have long kept the world back from progress.

In some passages the manner of presenting the truths here given may seem to border somewhat on the sarcastic; possibly on the blasphemous. Should any apology be needed for that, let it be found in the fact that the whole question, if it were not so ridiculous, would be a sublime sarcasm.

The clergy have been misrepresenting the devil; slandering the devil; libeling the devil and firing their heavy guns at the devil for over a thousand years; but they are very careful, in all they do, never to hit him, for they know that one effective blow dealt the devil in the right spot would stop all their business, and dry up the fountains of their support. The devil is truly the drive-wheel of theology. Ministers preach and pray and fast, and beg money, and take immense salaries, as God's especial agents to fight the devil. When they kill the devil there will be no one to tempt Christians—no one to lead astray—no one to sow Infidel or Spiritualistic doubts; in fact, there will be no further use for the church or its clergy. Rest assured, the clergy have seen the point, and hence they, in all their shots at the devil, have aimed to just miss him. This farce of the church and its ministry has, perhaps, caused me to, in places, seem unnecessarily sarcastic.

This pamphlet has been hastily written with the design of starting the reader to thinking in a rational manner on the questions introduced. If the devil, in these pages, has had his due, no one will be better satisfied than

THE AUTHOR.

Chicago, Jan. 16, 1890.

CHAPTER I.

THE CASE STATED.

WHAT MIGHT HAVE BEEN EXPECTED.—WHY THE DEVIL ARGUMENT IS POPULAR.—THE FACTS NOT DENIED.—NOT TRICKS—TESTIMONY OF A MINISTER.—THE ELECTRICITY ARGUMENT.—A CHEAP EXPLANATION— DO DEVILS WORK MIRACLES?—CAN DEVILS WORK MIRACLES?—A DILEMMA.—BIBLE PROVED TRUE BY THE DEVIL'S MIRACLES.

It was not to be expected that the churches and the ministers who have had a monopoly of guiding the religious thought of the world, would sit down and tamely submit to seeing themselves flanked by the spirit world, insomuch that the people in great numbers turn from them to the light of the spiritual philosophy, without entering some kind of protest. In their efforts to stop the onward march of the new religion, which, in the minds of the people, is rapidly supplanting the old, they will, of course, use the arguments which seem to them the most effectual.

To-day, the most common and popular resort of

the clergy in its opposition to Spiritualism, is to Rev. xvi:14:

"For they are the spirits of devils, working miracles, which go forth unto the kings of the earth, and of the whole world, to gather them to the battle of that great day of God Almighty."

I really see but little in the argument drawn from this text, unless it is that the sound of that horrible word, *devils*, is calculated to frighten a few who are moved by sound rather than by sense.

WHY THE POPULARITY OF THIS OBJECTION?

Why it is that this objection should become so popular with a certain class of ministers, I must frankly confess I cannot tell, unless it is for want of mental capacity to invest in objections which do not sound so loud, and yet really have much more weight.

Indeed, this is the only objection against Spiritualism which does not, in some way, place the *onus probandi* in the hand of the objector. Every other objection implies some knowledge and requires knowledge to back it up.

Let an objector, anywhere, or any time in the nineties, arise before an audience of twenty persons and undertake to argue that the facts do not occur, and he is liable to be met, not by fools and know-nothings, but by men and women of brains—honest men and women, who say to him, "Sir, you are mistaken; I know the manifestations occur, I have seen them." It takes a man more bold than wise to run against the united testimony of more than ten millions of witnesses. It is dangerous ground; few care to tread thereon.

ARE THEY TRICKS?

Should another step to the front and say, "Yes, the manifestations occur, but they are all tricks played by persons who pretend to be mediums." An editor in the city of New York steps to the front and says, "I have $10,000 deposited in the First National Bank of New York for you, when you explain, on the hypothesis of tricks, certain things I have seen and certain tests and communications which have come to me." He afterwards says: "I am authorized by certain capitalists to increase this offer to a round million."

No trickster takes the offer. Mediums are poor; they need the money; many of them are avaricious; they want the money, but they do not take this offer. The country is full of "exposers of Spiritualism," all of them after money, and yet none of them can be induced to accept this man's million dollars. I submit that that looks bad. It makes very thin ice for those to skate on who say Spiritualism is a trick.

On this point I am tempted to give the testimony

of one of the most popular opposers of Spiritualism in the world. Rev. Miles Grant, of Boston, in his "Spiritualism Unveiled," page 3, says:

"Some have assumed that all the manifestations of Spiritualism were the result of *trickery*, practiced by the mediums and those associated with them. This assumption might have answered very well in the early history of Spiritualism; but he who makes such a statement now would only show that *he knew but little about the facts in the case.* We think no one, after a little reflection, would venture to say of the many thousands, and even millions of Spiritualists, among whom are a large number of men and women noted for intelligence, honesty and veracity, that they are only playing tricks on each other; while, at the same time, they most boldly affirm that they are perfectly sincere in their belief that the manifestations come from the spirits of friends. Can anyone tell what object all these fathers, mothers, brothers, sisters, children, dear friends and loved companions, can have in pretending that they have communications from spirits, when they know, at the same time, that they are only deceiving each other by means of trickery? We think such a position is but little less than absurdity, and must be given up by those who would treat the subject with candor."

Such testimony as the foregoing needs but little comment; it is the testimony of one who is ransacking all creation to try to find something against Spiritualism. Surely, "Their rock is not as our rock, even our enemies themselves being the judges."

NOT ELECTRICITY.

Let still another say, It is electricity or it is *od force*; he implies certain knowledge of these forces which makes some explanation on his part necessary.

Men have spent a life-time studying electricity; they have taught it to carry messages through the land and under the sea; they have made it light our houses and our streets; they make it run our printing-presses and street-cars, but no one has, as yet, been able to make it talk, give tests, or manifest any other intelligence than comes through the operator at either end of the wires. So the best electricians in the world have said, No, electricity cannot produce or explain the Spiritual phenomena.

Thus the world, in its search for arguments against Spiritualism failed to find them until a class of cheap ministers came to the front and settled all questions by informing the world that

IT IS ALL DONE BY THE DEVIL.

If not by the old boss devil then by his myriads of subordinates who people the atmosphere surrounding our earth. When the minister is asked to explain this work of the devil, his answer, in substance, is, "How the devil do you suppose I know? the devil is a worker of miracles, and can do things beyond our power of explanation."

To prove that I have neither misapprehended nor misrepresented this matter, I quote again from Mr. Grant:

"They [the spirits] are deceiving men and women *by the means of miracles;* and leading a multitude to adopt doctrines of devils, instead of the truth of the Bible."

I have similar testimonies from other ministers, but this must suffice.

If the above position be true, the devil objection requires no argument; no outlay of brain force; no erudition; no logic. Educate a parrot to say "devil" and he at once becomes an eloquent and a faithful expounder of the opposition to Spiritualism!

HOW THEY KILL THE BIBLE.

The text "our friends, the enemy," quotes, says, "These are spirits of devils working miracles." Now, the devil is a worker of miracles or he is not. If he is not a worker of miracles then the text which says he is, is false; but if he is a worker of miracles then miracles cannot be used as the proof of any religion; for the very miracles used to prove the truth of a religion may have been wrought by his Satanic Majesty.

Ministers know the Bible is true; of course they do. But you ask them *how* they know it, and they will, every one of them, tell you, sooner or later, that they know it by the miracles which have been wrought in attestation of its truth.

At first it may not appear exactly clear how a miracle could prove the Bible true, or how a miracle could prove anything. How an ax floating on the water, or a man walking on the water, or three men enjoying a quiet sit down in the fire could prove anything more than that in the two former cases the ax and the man had lost their specific gravity, or the water had become more buoyant than usual, and in the latter that these men had more power to resist heat than usual, I cannot see. Suppose Jonah did live three days and three nights in the stomach of a fish; that only proves the diluted condition of the fish's gastric juice, or the weakness of his digestive apparatus, and leaves us to infer that he might have stayed a day or two longer or possibly taken up his permanent residence there—"only this and nothing more."

The miracles wrought by Moses, in Egypt, were, the most of them, duplicated by the Egyptians. We believe Moses beat them in the louse business. Probably it was too lousy a trick for the devil's agents to dabble in. Otherwise these miracles prove as much for the magicians as they do for Moses.

"No," says my clerical friend, "God alone has power to work miracles, and he never uses it except as a proof to the world that a certain message is from him. Miracles are given in confirmation of the Bible, and therefore prove it true."

Is that so? Then the text quoted is wrong. I repeat, the devil is, or he is not, a miracle worker! If he is a miracle worker then miracles do not prove the Bible true, for, he being a worker of miracles, may, for aught any one can know to the contrary, have wrought the very miracles by which the Bible is proved to be of divine origin. He is sharp enough to do that; and it would be exactly like one of his devilish tricks. Thus it is demonstrated that the devil is not a worker of miracles, or that miracles do not prove the Bible true.

But if the devil is not a worker of miracles, the text quoted above is false, for it says: "They are spirits of devils working miracles."

CHAPTER II.

DEMONS—WHAT ARE THEY?

ELDER GRANT ON DEMONS.—JOSEPHUS CONTRADICTS HIM.—ARE THEY SPIRITS OF THE DEAD?—THE GOOD AND BAD ALIKE ARE DEMONS.—IMPORTANT TESTIMONY FROM THE GREEKS.—JONES, CUDWORTH, LUCIANUS, ALEXANDER CAMPBELL, EURIPIDES, DR. GEO. CAMPBELL, DR. LARDNER, PHILO JUDÆUS AND OTHERS, ON DEMONS.

All agree that the word devil, in the text, "They are the spirits of devils," is the Greek word *daimoon*, commonly pronounced *demon*. I have three or four books before me now, written by the opposers of Spiritualism, which talk about Spiritualism being the work of demons. Mr. Grant, in the work to which I have before referred, says:

"The mistake of the Spiritualists, is in supposing that the 'familiar spirits' are human, instead of being demons, as the Bible shows."

It is the reverend gentleman himself, and not the Spiritualists, who are mistaken on this point. The Jews, to whom "were committed the oracles of

God," (Rom. iii:2) believed demons to be the spirits of dead men. John the Baptist, who went out under the influence of Elijah the prophet, (See Luke 1:17) was said by the Jews to be possessed of a demon. (Matt. xi:18.)

Josephus, who certainly understood the theology of the Jews and Romans, informed his readers that demons were spirits of the dead, both good and bad. In his "Wars," Book vii:, chapter 6, paragraph 3, he says:

"Yet after all his pains in getting, [a certain root] it is only valuable on account of one virtue it hath, that if it be only brought to the sick person, it quickly drives away those called demons, *which are none other than the spirits of the wicked that enter into men that are alive*, and kill them, unless they can obtain some help against them."

But Josephus and the Jews did not consider the demons all bad. He says in his "Wars of the Jews," Book vi: chapter 3, paragraph 5.

"For what man of virtue is there who does not know that those souls which are severed from the fleshly bodies in battles by the sword are received by the ether, that purest of elements, and joined to that company which are placed among the stars; and that *they become good demons and propitious heroes*, and show themselves as such to their posterity afterwards."

Maximus Tyrius says:

"What the multitude call death is but the beginning of immortality, and the birth into a future life. The soul, having put off this earthly body becomes a demon [*daimonion*], a word which, though employed only in an evil sense in the holy Scriptures, signifies among the

Greeks an intermediate being between men and gods and may be either good or evil." Dissert, 27.

Thus it seems that the Greeks, from whom the Jews learned the word, used it to signify departed human spirits.

The following dissertation on demons, I find prepared to my hand and have had it laid away so long that I have forgotten who compiled it. I, however, having examined the principal authorities, will vouch for its truth in every particular.

"*Demon* in the Greek, is *diamon*, to *know*, *a god*, used like Theos and Thea of individual *gods*. It is defined and used by scholars, lexicographers and classical writers, thus:

Jones—*Demon*, 'the spirit of a dead man.'
Cudworth—*Demon*, 'a spirit, either angel or fiend.'
Grote, the celebrated Grecian historian, declares that 'demons and gods were considered the same in Greece.'
Lucianus, a Greek writer, born at Samosata, in Syria, used *demon* in the sense of 'departed souls.'
Archbishop Whately says: 'The heathen authors allude to possession by a demon (or by a god, for they employ the two words with little or no distinction) as a thing of no uncommon occurrence.'

Alexander Campbell says:
'The demons of Paganism, Judaism and Christianity were spirits of dead men.'

Euripides, (Hipp. v, 141) makes the chorus address Phedra:

'Oh young girl, a *God* (demon) possesses thee; it is either Pan, or Hecate, or the venerable Corybantes or Cybele that agitates thee.'

Dr. Campbell says:
'All Pagan antiquity affirms that from Titan and

Saturn, the poetic progeny of Cœlus and Terra, down to Æsculapius, Proteus, and Minos, all their *divinities were ghosts of dead men*, and were so regarded by the most erudite of the Pagans themselves.'

Dr. Lardner writes:

'The notion of demons, or the souls of the dead, having power over living men, was *universally* prevalent among the heathen of those times, and believed by many Christians.'

Philo Judæus writes, (we quote from Yonge's Translation,) referring to the departed and immortalized:

'Which those among the Greeks that studied philosophy call *heroes and demons*, and which Moses, giving them a more felicitous appellation, calls *angels*, acting, as they do, the part of ambassadors, and messengers. Therefore if you look upon *souls*, and *demons*, and *angels*, as things differing indeed in name, but as meaning in reality one and the same thing, you will thus get rid of the heaviest of all difficulties, superstition. For the people speak of good demons and bad demons; so do they speak of good and bad souls. * * * Hence, the Psalmist David speaks of the 'operation of evil angels.''

Plato, speaking of a certain class of demons, says;

'They are demons because prudent and learned. * * * Hence, poets say when a good man shall have reached his end, he receives a mighty destiny and honor, and becomes a demon according to the appellation of prudence.'

Hesiod, in his 'Works and Days,' has these lines:

'But when concealed had destiny this race,
Demons there were, called *holy* upon earth,
Good, Ill-averters, and of Man the guard;
* * * * * * *
Holy demons by great Jove designed.'

Worcester, in his synonyms, says: 'Demon is sometimes used in a good sense; as, 'The demon of Socrates, or the demon of Tasso,—and then, to illustrate, quotes from that fine author, Addison: 'My good *demon*, who sat at my right hand during the course of this whole vision.' etc.

That learned *savant* Cardan, honored with the friendship of Gregory XIII, says: 'No man was ever great in any art or action, that did not have a demon to aid him.'"

This is enough to thoroughly reply to those who would scare the world away from Spiritualism with the word demon. The word being translated devils in the Bible, and being so universally associated with evil, people have scared at it. Hence, this chapter. Now, having removed this obstacle, reader and writer are prepared to enter upon the more direct argument.

CHAPTER III.

ORIGIN OF DEVILS.

THEY ARE DEMONS.—A MINISTER ON DEVILS.—REFLECTIONS ON THE SAME.—THE DEVIL'S FORMER POSITION.—BECAME DISSATISFIED.—WAR IN HEAVEN.—ARENA REMOVED TO EARTH.—THE DEVIL CAPTURES GOD'S MIRACLE TOOLS AND SETS UP BUSINESS.

I now ask, are these the spirits of devils working miracles? Should you take the classical idea of *demons*—the spirits of the dead, and drop the idea of miracles and simply say they were the spirits of the dead performing marvelous feats, I would not object; for that is just what they are. That Spiritualists preach; that their opponents deny. The opponents of Spiritualism treat the word devils, here as though these devils were the legitimate descendants of *Diabolus* or *Satan;* and, in handling the subject I shall be compelled to handle it with reference to that idea of the text.

With that view of the question we will seek to form the acquaintance of his Satanic Majesty and a few of his descendants; let us find out who made him, and when, and for what purpose—in short, let us "give the devil his due."

To accomplish this, we may go directly or indirectly back to some of the mythologies; we may strain our mythology through Christianity, or we may hand it out pure and unadulterated from contamination by passing under the hands of the John Milton's and the Ellen G. White's of Christianity.

A MINISTER ON THE DEVIL.

Rev. J. H. Waggoner, once one of the brightest lights in the personal devil firmament, presented the matter, in his "Nature and Tendency of Modern Spiritualism," as follows:

"As before said, we do not believe that God ever created a devil or a wicked man. But men exist, with the power and will to do evil. 'God made man upright,' but he became wicked by his own will and actions; and so of the devil. We hold that the only reasonable view is that of the Scriptures; that God creates intelligences, giving them power and freedom to act, without which they could form no character at all; and holds them accountable for the exercise of that power in the actions performed, and vindicates justice by bringing them to judgment. There are expressions in Ezek. xxviii, which can refer to no other being than the devil, by which we learn that he was created a 'covering cherub,' perfect and beautiful. But he fell because of pride. When Moses made the sanctuary, he was directed to make cherubim and place them on the mercy-seat over the ark, their wings overshadowing the mercy-seat. Heb. ix:5. The Lord promised to meet with them 'between the two cherubim.' Ex. xxv:22. As all this was a shadow and example of heavenly things, a visible representation of the sanctuary and true tabernacle in Heaven, which the Lord pitched, and not man, (Heb. viii:1-5; see also Ezek., chapters i-x,) we here learn the exalted position occupied, and consequently the great power possessed, by a covering cherub. In Ezek. xxviii, the prince of Tyrus is declared to be a man; the king of Tyrus was a covering cherub. This may well be applied to Satan, who is 'the prince of this world,' and who makes use of wicked earthly powers to accomplish his purposes; he was afterward represented by the Roman power, (Rev. xii), as it was then his special instrument of wickedness. He who is wise and strong to do good, will, of course, be wise and strong to do evil if he turns his powers in that direction. And as the cherubim in Heaven possess far more power than men, so if they fall, their power will be greater to do evil, in the same proportion. On this point we think it sufficient to add that the Scriptures affirm that angels have fallen; that there was more than human power exerted through the magicians of Egypt; and Satan is said to work miracles, 'with power, and signs, and lying wonders'."

Here man was made "upright" and the devil a "covering cherub;" but man has fallen, fallen, down, down, down, down, lower and still lower, until he has reached his present state of degradation, with prospects—nay, with prophecies that his tendency is still downward; and the devil, once a "covering cherub,"—one of the brightest, tallest, grandest angels God made, has fallen as much below man as he was created above man; and this devil still retains his power to work miracles, and by this power to hasten man down still farther, while the Gods and Christs and angels, yes, and even the ministers and prophets of the church have given up the miracle business altogether, and delivered all the tools into the hands of the hosts of darkness and of evil! Surely this is a dark picture, for God, Christ and his church! and there is no road open for poor, fallen and still descending humanity, but the "wide gate," and the "broad way, that leads to destruction." What a pity that God could not for a short time have the devil's power, or the devil could not have God's goodness, what a different world this would have been!

STORY OF THE ORIGIN OF DEVILS.

To comprehend the whole in one short story, all, or about all, who believe in a devil believe that he was made the grandest and "most noble Roman of them all." He was the finest specimen of—what shall I say—humanity or divinity? among all of God's offspring. God thought so much of him that he took him into his particular confidence— made him Secretary of State, as it were. In this God made no mistake, for everything went off well under Lucifer's administration. When the books were wanted for examination they were always on hand, ready to be examined; and they were always posted and correct. There were then no defalcations in heaven—no flights to Canada—there was no boodle—there were no heavenly boodlers—no Cronin murder cases—no jury bribing. In fact, there was nothing to mar, nothing to make afraid!

But for some reason a meeting was called of the heavenly cabinet and very important business transacted, probably nothing less than the creation of the planet on which we exist, which, it must be conceded, was important to us, and Satan, by some oversight, was not called to that meeting. Whether he was slighted on purpose, or whether it was an accident is not quite clear. But, be that as it may, Satan took umbrage; he felt that it was hardly a fair deal to make him responsible for all the business transacted in heaven and then to go on and transact the most important business without consulting him. He probably hinted his disaffection to a few of his most intimate friends, some of whom were not very good at keeping a secret.

The result was, the news of a little misunderstanding between Satan and God, got into the hands of the reporters and became so public that God sent to the devil, and told him that if he chose to tender his portfolio, his resignation would be accepted. But the devil determined not to resign under a cloud; he would wait until matters settled somewhat. God then peremptorily demanded his resignation, but Satan, feeling that "possession was nine points in law," obstinately refused; whereupon God commissioned Michael to go and take possession of the devil's books and office, at no matter what cost. But the devil had one-third of heaven armed and equipped for battle. John, in the Apocalypse, parodied heathen mythology as follows:

WAR IN HEAVEN.

"And there was war in heaven: Michael and his angels fought against the dragon; and the dragon fought and his angels, and prevailed not; neither was their place found any more in heaven. And the great dragon was cast out, that old serpent, called the devil, and Satan, which deceiveth the whole world; he was cast out into the earth, and his angels were cast out with him. * * * Therefore rejoice ye heavens, and ye that dwell in them. Woe to the inhabiters of the earth and of the sea; for the devil is come down unto you having great wrath because he knoweth that he hath but a short time." Rev. xii:7-12.

Happy had it been for the inhabitants of earth if the Gods and devils had either settled their quarrel or continued their "war in heaven;" but it seems that when the devils were cast out they were not conquered—the battle did not end. The only change was the removal of the *arena* from heaven to earth. Here the battle has been going on ever since.

This seems to me hardly fair. If the Gods and devils must fight; if they can't be induced to reform, let them keep their fight on the original battle-ground. Somehow they got tired of that and moved the *arena* from heaven to earth; and now, whatever the Gods and devils may think about it, the ministers persist in urging us into the battlefield. They call for us to volunteer and enlist in the Lord's army, and tell us, if we do not we will surely be drafted into the devil's army—fight, we must.

As I know but little about this God and devil quarrel, and as I am not a fighting man, I prefer to remain neutral and let those who know more about the matter fight it out. If I must fight, I propose to go into something of an investigation of the matter and cast my lot with the army which is in the right.

In this battle God has all the time had one advantage of the devil; it was not an honest advantage except on the ground that in war, as in love, everything is honorable. That is, whenever the devil got God into a tight place God would work himself out through a miracle. But now it seems that the devil has taken this last string out of the hands of the Omnipotent One. God has gone out of the miracle business entirely and the devil has picked up the tools where God laid them down and is now using them in the manufacture of spiritualistic miracles, for "they are the spirits of devils" working miracles.

CHAPTER IV.

A FEW MYTHOLOGICAL DEVILS AND HELLS.

A MINISTER ON FALLEN ANGELS.—WHAT AND WHERE IS HELL?—IS THE BIBLE THE WORK OF DEVILS?—TARTARUS, WHERE IS IT?—A THREE-STORY WORLD.—BRUNO UPSETS HEAVEN AND HELL.—GEOGRAPHY OF THE LAND OF THE NILE.—HOW PHENOMENA PRODUCED THE RELIGION OF EGYPT.—ORIGIN OF THE CROSS.—GODS CARRYING THE SUN.—HOW A NAUGHTY GOD GOT INTO TARTARUS.—TYPHON AND TYPHOID FEVER.

In one of my debates with Rev. Miles Grant, of Boston, he used, as nearly as I can remember, the following language:

"I will save my friend the trouble of presenting further proof that the spiritual phenomena occur, by admitting them all. That they occur there can be no doubt. Indeed, we not only have indisputable testimony that they do occur, but we have testimony of the Bible that they shall occur. But they are not produced by the spirits of the dead. 'The dead know not anything.' They are 'spirits of devils working miracles'—fallen angels which kept not their first estate—wicked spirits in high places. Peter says, 'God spared not the angels that sinned, but cast them down to hell.' These fallen angels, cast down to hell are the ones who produce the phenomena of Spiritualism."

When I met him with the thought that that would involve the idea of a hell of fire and brimstone, a thing which he denied, his reply was, in substance, as follows:

"No, there are three words in the Greek Testament rendered hell; one is *Hades*, which signifies the place or the state of the dead. Another is *Gehenna*, which was a valley just south of Jerusalem, where a fire was kept continually burning to cremate the filth of the city; and the other was *Tartarus* or *Tartarosus*, which signifies earth's lower atmosphere, or the atmosphere immediately surrounding the earth. This is the word occurring in 2 Peter ii:14, where the angels are cast down to hell, and this is the only place where the word occurs in the Bible. Paul refers to the same thing in Eph. vi:12, where he speaks of 'spiritual wickedness in high places,' or wicked spirits in the atmosphere."

Those who have read Mr. Grant's writings, or heard him preach, will testify that I have not misrepresented him. Now for the reply.

If this gentleman, and those of his way of thinking, are correct, only fallen angels get into hell; but as hell means earth's atmosphere, only fallen angels get into earth's atmosphere! Jesus says: "I could pray to my father and he would send me more than twelve legions of angels," but as angels could not have approached Jesus without getting into hell, that is, into earth's atmosphere, the angels sent by his father could have been none other than fallen angels. When Jesus prayed there appeared an angel unto him, strengthening him. But as this angel came *en rapport* with earth's atmosphere, in order to reach Jesus, he must have been a devil!

Stephen says: "The law was given by the disposition of angels." But as none but fallen angels get into earth's atmosphere, the angels who gave the law must have been devils. Thus the Bible, as well as Spiritualism, is proved to be of demoniacal origin.

But the theory is wrong; hell—*tartarus*—does not signify earth's atmosphere, but a lake of supposed fire and brimstone. To find its origin we will be compelled to look up

SOME OF THE PRE-HISTORIC MYTHOLOGIES.

All these things can be traced back to Egypt, probably no further. There our gods and devils, and, in fact, all our religious beliefs were born.

Religions, gods, devils and hells were born of certain phenomena in nature. The old religions do not fit our knowledge to-day. The thing called religion was fitted to a flat world—an earth that had corners and ends. The fact is, before the discoveries of science, when we had no other guide than religion, the universe was a

THREE-STORY AFFAIR.

We commenced our existence here, on the second story; if we did pretty well, when we got through with this story God opened the windows of heaven and took us up through the window to his apartment in the third story. If we were naughty here, the devil, who was only another god, opened the trapdoor and took us into the sub-cellar to his apartments. That his apartments were filled with fire could be proved by the volcanoes belching out fire and smoke.

Any minister, in former times, could point to God and heaven; all he had to do was to point up. He was equally as successful in pointing to the devil and hell; all he had to do was to point downward.

Since Giordano Bruno demonstrated the rotundity and the revolution of the earth, the church cannot be quite so certain about the exact location of either place. A minister preaching in America and a missionary preaching in China at the same time, in pointing to heaven would point in opposite directions; and in pointing to hell would point at each other. The result is they are all at sea about the location of either of these places, and had they "the wings of a dove" so that they could "fly away and be at rest," they would be as likely to light in Pluto's dominions as in the other place. The wisest men now do not know which way "up" and "down" are. No wonder the church burned Bruno at the stake. He knocked the bottom out of an orthodox hell, and, at the same time, knocked the particular heaven of these good people into *pi*.

THEOLOGY AND MYTHOLOGY.

As chemistry grew out of alchemy, and astronomy grew out of astrology, so theology grew out of mythology. Our theological ideas can all be traced back to the early mythologies in the valley of the Nile.

A little knowledge of geography would do no harm; in fact, it might assist in understanding this subject. Egypt is a long strip of country, some places very narrow and some places wider, lying on either side of the river Nile, extending from Alexandria on the Mediterranean, at the mouth of the Nile, up to Ipsamboul, near one thousand miles south of Alexandria.

The Nile beween these two places is without a tributary. Not a river, creek or rivulet enters it for over *one thousand miles*. Formerly, it very seldom, or perhaps never, rained in Egypt. Since the Suez Canal has been completed from the Dead Sea to the Mediterranean, occasional showers pass up and down the canal.

It can be proven that the Nile, for not less than seventy-five thousand years, has annually overflowed the banks and inundated nearly or quite all of Egypt. The river has made its record depositing its layer of *debris* topping it off with the red mud of Nubia, for over one hundred thousand years.

Now go back as far as mythology will carry us and you will learn that the Nile came up every year, and that without rain or any other visible cause, and swept everything before it. In course of time, persons were selected to investigate the cause of these phenomena and report. These investigators, by watching the stars, soon learned that they were regular, and that when certain stars appeared they might look for a flood. They soon divided the zodiac, that is the path of the sun from the extreme north to the extreme south, into twelve compartments; called now the twelve signs of the zodiac. They learned in which compartment the flood came, so that they could not only say, "For yet seven days and I will bring a flood of water upon the whole earth," but they could proclaim the flood as Noah did, one hundred and twenty days beforehand.

After a few thousand years, when it was learned just when the Nile was expected to rise, and how high it was expected to come, and if people would stack their grain and build their houses above high water mark they would be safe, they sent engineers all over the country to erect crosses of wood and stone to tell people how high to put the bottom of their buildings.

A Christian historian by the name of Socrates, supposes that a superstitious people after learning that the Nile usually came to the cross and never above it, concluded that there was some power in the cross to keep the Nile down, and thus was developed a kind of worship of the cross thousands of years before Jesus was crucified upon a cross. Thus the Christian cross originated in the valley of the Nile.

But it was my intention, had I not been switched off, to give you something of an idea of devils and hells.

When our earth was flat, long before the discoveries of science, the sun rose in the east and set in the west, as it appears to do now. The laws of gravitation had not been discovered; the centripetal and the centrifugal forces were unknown, so unless there were some gods, (devils, for they are all one,) connected with the matter, the sun would be liable to fall to the earth at any time, and the falling of so large a lump of fire as the sun, on any part of our large earth would be liable to do some damage.

Gods in those days did everything. The time was when God picked our apples and threw them down to the ground; and when Sir Isaac Newton discovered the laws of gravitation, a learned Christian bishop said such discoveries would drive God out of the world. He was right. Anthropomorphic, miracle-working deities are driven into very close quarters.

Well, in the days above spoken of, a god by the name of Phæton loaded the sun into his carriage in the morning and drove over the heavens with it from east to west, when he got to the western end of his journey he unloaded it into *tartarus*, hell, and it floated back through the stream to the place where it started from. In the night Phæton had driven back, and the next morning he again loaded up the red-hot sun and started on another trip; this he continued to do until he was discharged and another god by the name of Typhon or Typho, was given the job. This Typhon, was a young, wild, erratic god, utterly incapable of taking old trusted Phæton's place; but, like many others, he was always wanting to perform the impossible; so he teased his father to let him drive the horses which pulled the sun.

One day he did some wonderful act, which caused his father to swear by the god Osiris, who sleeps in Phile, that he would grant Typhon any request he might ask. Typhon, upon hearing this, renewed his request to drive Phæton's horses. The sun was accordingly loaded into the carriage and Typhon was mounted on the seat and the lines put into his hands; he had not driven far when the horses made the discovery that they did not have their old driver, whereupon they made a dash for earth, and brought the sun so near that they came near burning it up. Probably this dreadful calamity would have happened, had not Jupiter at this time been in Vulcan's shop forging thunderbolts. He saw what was going on and picked up a handful of these bolts and hurled them through Typhon, killing him. He then took the lines and attended to the moving of the sun himself until the rotundity of the earth and its gravitation were discovered.

When Typhon was killed he was put into *tartarus*, that portion of it which was located in Lake Avernus, I think. The exact location of Lake Avernus, and Surbonus and other mythological places, are like Sodom and Gomorrah, hard to determine. But they were somewhere in what was once the valley of the Nile. These lakes had neither outlet nor inlet. The water came in by the overflow of the Nile and passed out by evaporation.

Decaying vegetation in the region of these lakes gave the smell of brimstone, and the rolling of the waves in the light of the moon caused the lake to look like a huge lake of fire. Huge phosphoric insects flying over the lakes looked like balls of fire, or sparks from the lake.

A slow fever, generated by the poisonous miasma arising from the lake, was supposed to be an infliction from the god Typhon, confined in the bottom of that lake; hence it is to this day called *typhus or typhoid* fever.

This god grew and increased in strength so that it was dangerous to keep him where he was, although he was supposed to be thoroughly secured, so they set a couple of mountains down on him to hold him down; and for thousands of years when these gods—for there were many of them confined there for various reasons—grew restive in their chains and tried to break out of their prison, Vesuvius and Etna belched out fire and smoke.

Here, readers, is as far as I have been able to trace the origin of your devils and hells—here *tartarus* was born. And when Peter referred to *tartarus* he referred to this story of heathen mythology.

Now, having pursued this matter as far as space will permit, I will close this chapter, and open one on the works of devils.

CHAPTER V.

THE DEVIL AS A REFORMER.

THE CHURCH AND THE DEVIL.—WHERE THE FACTS USED CAN BE FOUND.—DEVILS IN JOHN AND JESUS.—DEVILS IN REFORMERS.—GILES COREY.—DEVILS IN FOLKS, WINDMILLS AND STEAMBOATS.—THE DEVIL AND DEATH IN THE SAWMILL.—GALILEO AND THE DEVIL.—CHURCH ARGUMENTS.—A CHURCH REVIEW'S APOLOGY.—THE PRINTING-PRESS.—JENNER.—THE DEVIL IN GEOLOGY.—HUGH MILLER'S TRAGIC DEATH.—THE DEVIL AS AN ABOLITIONIST.—WILL SUCCEED AS A SPIRITUALIST.

If the church has been a proper judge there has never been a reformer in the world who has not in some way been connected with the devil. The church has always claimed the same authority to judge for the world it now claims; it was, in past ages, thought to be more nearly infallible than it is to-day. Hell has been the grand store-house of reforms and the *rendezvous* of reformers. Reference to a few of the most common historical facts will prove this.

References to many of the facts used in this chapter, are, at present writing, quite out of my reach. I am writing this on a train which carries me farther every moment from my books; but if the reader will get a book called "The Healing of the Nations," and read the introduction, written by Senator Talmage, he will find many of them; if he can procure a monthly magazine called "The Examiner," published by Edward C. Towne, in Chicago, I think in 1868, he will there find a paper translated from the French, which gives many more facts than are here presented. For other sources of information consult Lecky, Buckle, Draper and the Encyclopedias.

THE DEVIL IN JOHN AND JESUS.

John the Baptist and Jesus were both accused of being in league with the devil. Of John they said: "Behold he hath a devil." They said of Jesus: "Thou art a Samaritan and hast a devil." They said: "He casteth not out devils but by Beelzebub, the prince of devils." To those who were led away by his doctrines, they said: "Why hear ye him, he hath a devil?"

Thus, according to the concensus of the popular church of their day John and Jesus each had some mysterious connection with the devil. But the church to-day will acknowledge that, devil or no devil, John and Jesus were in the right and the church in the wrong; and whatever their practice may be, they will profess to be followers of those accused of being under the influence of devils rather than to be the legitimate descendants of their accusers.

If the church is infallible John and Jesus did their work by the power of devils; but if the church made a mistake then I will consider that it is liable to err, and will look as often as twice before I shall conclude that the devil is in Spiritualism, on the mere *ipse dixit* of pulpit ignoramuses.

THE DEVIL IN THE DARK AGES.

Lack of space and a legitimate want of patience on the part of many of my busy readers will prevent me from retrospectively traveling through the Dark Ages, or I could show you that every reformer was the devil's especial vicegerent, during all that time. I remember of reading in Edward C. Towne's "Examiner," a scrap of history translated from the French, stating that *five thousand* children under the age of five years, were put to death by the Catholic church for being emissaries of the devil. If a child manifested any precocity in any particular direction it was supposed the devil was operating through the child as he did through the snake in the garden, and the child was put to death.

Giles Corey, of Salem witchcraft fame, on two occasions manifested wonderful feats of physical strength; this was proof to Cotton Mather, Sir Matthew Hale and others that he was a wizzard, possessed of the devil, and he was pressed to death.

When the common flesh fork was invented it was bitterly denounced by the clergy. One minister warned his audience that God would resent the indignity of refusing to take their meat in their fingers by palsying the hand that took up one of these infernal inventions of the devil. Church history was called into requisition to prove that God had always in the past resented similar insults.

When an old Scotchman invented the fanning-mill—a machine to separate chaff from wheat—an old Scotch lady, by advice of her pastor, took her son Coody away from the man. The charge brought against the man was that he was irreverently trying to raise the devil's wind. The advice given by the clergy was, when you want to separate wheat and chaff, get down on your knees and humbly ask God to send you a good dispensation of air. If you have not the humility to pray for wind, at least have the patience to wait for it. Raising the devil's wind was a presumption not to be tolerated.

The wind-mill, however, was perfected; and contrary to church prophecies, it worked; and contrary to church prophecies, God did not manifest signs of displeasure. Presbyterians even ate of the bread, made of the wheat which had been separated from the chaff by the devil's wind. The church could not tolerate such impiety as that; these persons were promptly excommunicated, and delivered over to the tender mercies of his Satanic Majesty. The devil was right, and the church wrong in the case of the fork and wind-mill. How is it elsewhere?

When Robert Fulton invented the steamboat, the church everywhere prophesied against it; it would not work; or, if it did, it was an insult to Almighty God, and the work of the devil to run a boat against God's wind and tide. One English clergyman, in preaching against Robert Fulton and his steamboat, proposed to eat the first steamboat and everybody and everything on board, that ever ventured into British waters. Boats have gone there, and to-day England owns more of them than all the world besides, but who ever heard of this Englishman performing his vow.

THE DEVIL IN THE SAW-MILL.

The next stronghold of the devil was in Germany; the former method of sawing lumber was to put a log upon a scaffolding, and one man take his position under the log and another on top; one pulled the saw down and the other pulled it up. The thought occurred to one man that a little mountain stream near by could be utilized to turn a flutter-wheel, a crank could be fixed to the wheel, a shaft to the crank and a saw to the shaft, and thus a great amount of manual labor could be saved. He went to work and built his mill and was put to death for it.

God had said: "In the sweat of thy face shalt thou eat bread;" but this was a labor-saving machine; man did not half sweat sitting with his arms folded and watching the water saw his lumber. This invention if not rebuked, would be followed by other labor-saving inventions, and thus God Almighty's curse would be thwarted. The man who invented it did it by the aid of the devil and was put to death.

A NINETEENTH CENTURY FOSSIL.

This reminds me of an occurrence in Cincinnati in the autumn of 1869. A Baptist minister announced in the Saturday papers that he would preach on the oil speculation, on Sunday night. In the course of his sermon he gave as one evidence that the devil was in the oil business, the fact that God had prophesied that the "elements shall melt with fervent heat; the earth also, and all that is therein shall be burned up." He then told his hearers that God had wisely deposited coal in certain places in the earth, with which to burn it; but coal being rather hard to kindle, God had wisely deposited millions upon millions of barrels of crude oil in the vicinity of his coal deposits to serve as kindling-wood, to set the coal on fire. The culmination was: Now, the devil has set the infidels to tapping God's oil can, so that when the time comes to burn the world, it won't burn worth a d———.

This minister was born three hundred years too late; he was a fifteenth century man. I treat all such men as I would any other fossil.

When, in the sixteenth century, Galileo came to the conclusion that the earth was round, and was one of numerous worlds, many of which were probably inhabited, he was denounced as being in league with the devil; not only by the Catholic Church, but by Martin Luther himself.

The arguments used against Galileo were stated *seriatim* as follows:

1. "It casts suspicion on the doctrine of Incarnation.
2. It upsets the whole foundation of Theology.
3. If the earth is only one among many planets, then other planets must be inhabited, and if so, all men did not descend from Adam, or Noah."

The above and other similar arguments were quite sufficient to prove to Catholics and Protestants alike that Galileo was in partnership with the devil.

Andrew D. White, to whom I am indebted for many of the facts in this chapter, says:

"When Galileo had discovered the four satellites of Jupiter, the whole thing was denounced as impossible and impious. It was argued that the Bible clearly showed, by all applicable types, that there could be only seven planets; that this was proved by the seven golden candlesticks of the Apocalypse, by the seven branched candlesticks of the tabernacle, and by the seven churches of Asia. * * * Mathematical and other reasonings were met by the words of Scripture. * * * It was declared that Galileo's doctrine was proved false by the standing still of the sun for Joshua; by the declaration that the foundations of the earth are fixed so firm that they cannot be moved; and that the sun runneth about from one end of heaven to the other."

While Luther, in Protestant Wittenberg, was preaching against Galileo, the Dominican Father at Rome, Caccini, was issuing his invectives from Rome. He preached on the text, "Why stand ye gazing up into heaven?" In that sermon, White says:

"He insisted that geometry is of the devil; and that mathematicians should be banished, as the author of all heresies."

Mr. White proceeds as follows:

"For the final assault, the park of heavy artillery was at last wheeled into place. *You see it in all the scientific battle-fields. It consists of general denunciation.* * * * It was brought to bear on Galileo with this declaration.
The opinion of the earth's motion, is, of all heresies, the most abominable, the most pernicious, the most scandalous. The immobility of the earth is thrice sacred. The argument against the immortality of the soul, the creator, the incarnation, etc., should be tolerated sooner than an argument to prove that the earth moves."

Galileo urged his accusers to look through his telescope and be convinced, but they refused. One Calvius declared that the devil had enabled Galileo to invent an instrument to distort man's vision and make things appear as they were not.

Poor Galileo was imprisoned and abused almost beyond description for his heresy, and finally compelled to get down on his knees before church authority and say:

"I, Galileo, being in my seventieth year, being a prisoner, and on my knees, and before your eminences, having before my eyes the holy gospel, which I touch with my hands, *abjure, curse and detest* the heresy of the movement of the earth."

The devil, Galileo and science were right; God, the Bible and the church were wrong, as usual. Now, who is to blame for this conflict? On this point, "The Dublin Review" says:

"But it may be well doubted whether the church did oppose scientific truth. What retarded it was the circumstance that *God thought fit to express many texts of Scripture in words which have every appearance of denying the earth's motion. But it is God who did this, not the church;* and, moreover, since he thought fit to so act as to *retard the progress of truth,* it would be little to her discredit, even if she followed his example."

What a confession! God, the Bible and the church all against the truth; and only the devil and a poor old man to advocate it. But the devil and Galileo succeeded. Well may the poet say:

"Keep, Galileo, to thy thought,
   And nerve thy soul to bear;
They may gloat o'er the senseless words they wring
   From the pangs of thy despair;
They veil their eyes but they cannot hide
   The sun's meridian glow;
The heel of a priest may tread thee down,
   And a tyrant work thee woe;
But never a truth has been destroyed;
   They may curse it and call it a crime,
And pervert, and betray, or slander and slay
   Its teachers for a time.
But the sunshine, aye, shall light the sky
   As round and round we run,
And the truth shall ever come uppermost,
   And justice shall be done."

PRINTING-PRESS.—JENNER.—GEOLOGY.

The printing-press was once the **work of the devil**. A Catholic priest prophesied that if this thing went on the vulgar [common] people would demand that the Bible be printed and somebody would print it; it would thus become a vulgar book, and people would lose their respect for it. In this he was partially, if not wholly, correct. The sacredness of Bibles and the frightfulness of devils each vanish as people get on more intimate terms with them.

When Thomas Jenner accidently discovered that vaccination took the deadly sting out of small-pox, he was denounced in long printed statements as having formed a partnership with the devil to turn man back to the *genus quadrumane*. It was even asserted where vaccination was not known, that horns were sprouting on the heads of vaccinated children. Hundreds of stories were published as silly as any told about Spiritualism, to prove vaccination was of the devil. But in this, as in other instances, the devil was in the right and the church in the wrong.

GEOLOGY AND THE DEVIL.

I remember well the beginning of the controversy on geology. The clergy, led by Moses Stewart and other prominent New England pulpiteers, denounced geology as the devil's religion, and geologists as agents of his Satanic Majesty. I remember, when, as a child, I was afraid to meet a geologist; geologists were all of the devil, and geology was the devil's Bible. After awhile, Prof. Agassiz became a geologist; then it began to grow a little more respectable. Later, Hugh Miller, a Scotch stone-cutter and a Christian, became a geologist and produced two books.

"Foot-prints of the Creator," and "Old Red Sandstone," were, in the estimation of the church, destined to convert and baptize geology. Miller's works were heralded to the world as the great antidote to "Infidel geology." They satisfied nearly every Christian except their author. He wrote again and again. Finally he was to bring out his biography and in that was to forever settle the question as to geology; this work was to exorcise the demons from geology.

But Mr. Miller was not to finish his book. If you could have seen him and read his thoughts one dark November night in 1855, you would have found him wrestling with himself. His Bible was telling him one story and stalactites, stalagmites, conglomerates and fossils were telling him another. What was he to do? Harmonize them he could not. He knew the "sermons in stones" were true; he had been listening to them and interpreting them for many years; they had never lied to him. He could not make them agree with the story he read in Genesis. Finally, in despair at not being able to make the Bible and geology harmonize, he picked up a pistol and sent a ball through his heart. He sent himself to the country where these questions are settled, because he could not harmonize God's and the devil's Bibles. He knew geology was true, and if the devil was the author he was the author of truth.

Oh, Christian, I bring the bleeding corpse of this man and throw it at your feet, and hurl the charge upon you that you have bathed your hands in the blood of this man. You, in forcing him to attempt what no man can do, drove him to fill a suicide's grave. To-day, geology is not of the devil. Prof. Dawson, one of the greatest Christians in the world, is the greatest geologist in the world.

THE DEVIL IN ABOLITIONISM.

The next you hear of the devil is, he is in the antislavery movement. As a boy, I was often warned by the ministers that the devil was in the abolition movement. God and the Bible were in favor of slavery; the devil was trying to overthrow God's precious law, by repealing the clause which says, "Cursed be Caanan," etc.

Every church in Christendom denounced the abolitionists, and said slavery was a divine institution, until Infidels and heretics carried it on to success. (I have in my possession to-day, books containing the resolutions passed by all the leading churches in favor of the divinity of slavery and against fire-eating infidel abolitionists.) The abolition ball had long been rolling up hill; the church had either been fighting the work or standing by and looking listlessly on until the whole world saw it was bound to be a success in spite of all opposition, when they rushed to the work with a "Come on, boys, give it one more roll! Heave, oh, heave." Then, when they saw the thing descending the inclined plane of public opinion propelled by its own weight, they turn to the world and say, "See what we've done."

(Now, if the devil has carried all the works I have mentioned, on to success, he has in that given us a sufficient guarantee of the success of Spiritualism. If the devil is in Spiritualism, as he has been in every other reform, the ministers may as well learn from the past and surrender. They are ours.) The only trouble with them will be when they come over in a body, as they will do, they will all claim that they always were Spiritualists, and it will be about impossible to find one who did not see from the start that God was in Spiritualism; and together they will shout the chorus, The church did it.

CHAPTER VI.

DEVILS IN THE BIBLE.

AN HONORABLE DEVIL.—WHERE THE JEWS GOT THEIR DEVIL.—A TEMPTING GOD.—ALLEGORY OF THE FIRST ELEVEN CHAPTERS OF GENESIS.—WOMAN AN AFTERTHOUGHT.—HOW SHE WAS MADE.—THE DEVIL TAKES THE FIELD.—HE TOLD WOMAN WHAT GOD HAD SAID.—DEVIL IMPARTS WISDOM.—THE CURSE UPON THE DEVIL FAILS.—THE DEVIL BEATS GOD IN JOB'S CASE.—CONCLUSION.

I have given you a *resume* of the devil's work in mythology and in history; it remains for me to briefly trace his work through the Bible. As the devil was not so bad in mythology as one might imagine, and, as in history he was always right; and, no matter what the opposition, always successful, so the reader may anticipate that in the Bible he was always truthful and reformatory. I say, truthful, though Jesus said he was "a liar and the father of it." Jesus also accused him of being a "murderer from the beginning," yet, on his behalf, I deny the charge. He never killed anybody—never harmed anybody. The first the Bible knows of the devil was when "that old serpent, which is the devil and

Satan," came to the woman in the Garden of Eden. Indeed, this devil was not called anything but a serpent until in the very last part of the New Testament. John tells us twice that the "old serpent" is the devil and Satan. Rev. xii:9, and xx:2.

The fact is, the Jews knew nothing of any devils, great or small, old or young, until after the Babylonists' captivity.

A TEMPTING GOD.

In Abraham's day, a tempting devil had not been introduced among the Jews, so there was no other way than for God to do his own tempting. Thus in Gen. xxii:1, we read:

"And it came to pass after these things that God did tempt Abraham."

After the devil was introduced to do the tempting business, James said:

"Let no man say when he is tempted, I am tempted of God; for God cannot be tempted with evil, neither tempteth he any man." James i:13.

In 2 Samuel xxiv:1, the writer says:

"And again the anger of the Lord was kindled against Israel, and he moved David against them to say, Go, number Israel and Judah."

Here, as in Abraham's case, God attends to the tempting business himself, but this story is told again after they had been introduced to a few of the Babylonian devils, and there is no God in the temptation only as he employs the other fellow. In 1 Chron. xxi:1, we read:

"And Satan stood up against Israel and provoked David to number Israel."

Here Satan is doing God's work if God did not do Satan's in the previously quoted passage. This is two accounts of the same temptation.

CREATION.—GOD FORGETS TO MAKE A WOMAN.

Now, I will trace through the Bible a few of the acts of the devil. As the story goes, for, be it remembered, everything in the Bible prior to the call of Abraham, is allegory, when God made and furnished the world, he made everything in pairs except man; he only made one of the human species. In fact, he did not discover for some time that it was "not good for man to be alone." He seemed to entirely forget to make a woman. This is not strange as there are three persons in the Godhead, every one of them of the "masculine persuasion," and bachelors; an "innumerable company of angels," all he; "legions of devils," all of the same gender. It is no wonder that it was supposed that man could get along in a state of "single blessedness," and woman was left off the regular creation-program. But God was not long in making the discovery that "it is not good for man to be alone," and as an afterthought, woman was introduced. But how was she to be brought into the world, was the question; creation was finished, the material used up, and there was no woman. God was not long in coming to the conclusion that enough could be spared out of man to build up a woman, so he puts the young man to sleep and goes to work to manufacture for him, and out of material furnished by him, a wife. The story was as follows:

"And the Lord God caused a deep sleep to fall upon Adam, and he slept; and he took one of his ribs, and closed up the flesh instead thereof; and the rib which the Lord God had taken from man, made he a woman, and brought her unto the man. And Adam said, this is now bone of my bones, and flesh of my flesh, she shall be called woman, because she was taken out of man!" Gen. ii:21-23.

Robert G. Ingersoll represents God as standing there with that rib in his hand, the blood dripping from it, and asking himself the question, "Now, shall I make a blonde or a brunette of this?"

THE DEVIL IN THE ARENA.

Now, the devil steps in and begins his work on woman. God had said to man before woman was made:

"Of every tree of the garden thou mayest freely eat except the tree of knowledge of good and evil that grows in the midst of the garden; of that thou shalt not eat, for in the day thou eatest thereof, thou shalt surely die."

Adam probably never thought to mention to his wife that the fruit of that tree was poison. She never would have heard of it had it not been for the devil, who came to her and told her what God had said to her husband; but he told her ye shall not surely die, for God doth know that in the day ye eat thereof then your eyes shall be opened and ye shall become as gods, knowing good and evil.

Now, if there was anything in the world that our grandmother Eve wanted, it was wisdom. This is dreadful!

"And when the woman saw it was good for food, and that it was pleasant to the eyes, and a tree to be desired to make one wise, she took of the fruit thereof and did eat."

It is here clear that the woman ate of the fruit and gave it to her husband because she wanted wisdom; and she got wisdom by this act, there can be no doubt. The Bible says, "And the eyes of them both were opened, and they knew that they were naked." Even God is reported to have acknowledged that by this act, *"Man is become as one of us to know good and evil."* Thus, it is clear that God's aim was to keep man ignorant, and the devil's aim to give him wisdom. The devil was right, and thanks to his perseverance, he succeeded!

GOD CURSES.

Now God is foiled; he did not learn of the matter until near sundown of that day. "He walked out in the cool of the day." It seems that Adam and Eve either saw the Lord or heard him walking and "hid themselves because they were naked." Yes, *hid from Omnipresence*. After God failed to find them he called and they "came out," and God proceeded to "curse." He cursed Adam with the ability to perspire. I am glad of this curse, it enables us to throw off effete matter, and renew our youth.

He next cursed woman; he tells her that her desire shall be to her husband. What a dreadful curse! But I fear that some women are not badly cursed. I have seen women that I thought loved almost anybody else's husband better than they did their own. He then threatens to multiply her children. How do I know but that I am indebted to the devil for my existence? Yes, on the whole, I am glad the devil raised a rumpus and beat God in the garden.

God then turns upon the devil and begins his curse there; he tells him he shall crawl on his belly and eat the dust. Does that refer to the serpent, or to the devil? If to the snake, how did he move before the curse? Did he walk without legs, or fly without wings? Does the serpent eat dust? No, he eats less dust than any other living thing unless it is a fish. Is it the devil who is thus cursed? Yes, in this is the whole point. And the devil was to crawl all the days of his life, was he? Well, he is a progressive being; he will not crawl long. He crawls until he gets out of the sight of God, then he gets up and walks like other folks.

After this God and the devil did not meet for some thousands of years; at last they chanced to meet in heaven. The devil had been kicked out of heaven, but by some means he got back. There are two accounts, one in the first and the other in the second chapter of Job.

"The sons of God came to present themselves before the Lord, and Satan came also." When God saw the devil, he said, "Satan, whence comest thou?" The devil got up and strutted across the room and said, "From going to and fro in the earth, and from *walking* up and *down* in it."

Do you see that he is not crawling as much as he was? This language of the devil reminds God of his defeat in the garden, and God virtually confessing his defeat in that case, refers to Job; he says, "Hast thou considered my servant, Job? there is none like him in all the earth, a perfect and upright man." Implying that you could not fool him as you did Adam.

The devil replies that, "Job doth not serve God for naught," then tells God what he has done for him. God acknowledges it all, but thinks Job would serve him just the same if he had not done anything; but even now were he to cease to do for him, and were even the devil to be turned loose on him with all manner of afflictions, even yet Job would serve God. The devil thinks he would curse God to his face.

The upshot was, that Job was put into the hands of the devil, and was afflicted by his Satanic Majesty, and under God's direction. The next thing known of Job he was cursing till the air was perfectly blue. The Bible says, "Job opened his mouth and cursed his day." He cursed the stars, cursed his mother, cursed the one who brought news of his birth—in fact, cursed everything.

The devil had beaten God again, as he had done before.

The next you hear of the devil he is an "angel of light." Then he gets so far along that certain ones, when all other sources fail, are "delivered over to Satan for the destruction of the flesh, that the spirit may be sound in the day of grace." Alexander, the coppersmith, was delivered over to the devil that he might learn not to blaspheme.

Now, I ask, where has the devil done anything wrong in all this? Am I not right in saying he is a reformer and a progressionist? A thousand things can be truthfully said against the orthodox God, but not one against its devil.

CHAPTER VII.

WHY DOES THE DEVIL EXIST?—IS THIS BLASPHEMY?—REV. MILES GRANT'S OPINION.—REPLY.—MY CONTINUAL PRAYER.—ITS ANSWER.—HAS GOD SENT DEVILS IN ANSWER TO MY PRAYER?—WHY DON'T GOD KILL THE DEVIL?—"THE DEVIL IS DEAD."

WHY DOES THE DEVIL EXIST?

The statements in the last chapter about the devil, perhaps sounded blasphemous to many who have been taught to look upon the devil with holy horror. I intended they should. Some readers need shocking to wake them up. I will now tell you why I have said all this.

I have no idea of the existence of the devil. He has no existence save in the superstitious ignorance of the unthinking multitude. Where knowledge goes, devils flee. As the light of science supplants mediæval ignorance and superstition, devils, goblins and satyrs are forced into closer and darker quarters.

In a debate on Spiritualism, my opponent, Rev. Miles Grant, of Boston, said, in substance, the following:

"That Mr. Hull is under the influence of spirits, there can be but little doubt among those who hear him, but, he is controlled by the spirits of devils. Satan, who has the power to 'transform himself into an angel of light,' is deceiving Mr. Hull, and leading him on to 'swift destruction.' Mr. Hull was once a preacher of righteousness, but, alas! the devil has got him."

I answered: If I am under the influence of devils, *woe be to your God*. As my respondent has said, twelve of the best years of my life were spent in preaching what he terms the gospel; whether I was an able and eloquent minister or not you can learn by consulting anyone who ever heard me. Whether I was honest in my preaching no one can positively know except myself. I preached my opponent's gospel because *I believed* it—for no other reason in the world. I ceased preaching it because I could no longer believe it.

All this time I was a praying man. Never a day passed but that from three to ten times I got down on my knees, in my secret closet; at the family altar; in the pulpit; wherever I was, and prayed. The greatest burden of my prayer was, "O Father, give me thy holy spirit."

Hundreds of times I have fallen upon my knees before God in prayer, and while in prayer I have opened my Bible to Luke xi:11-13, and read:

"If a son shall ask bread of any of you that is a father, will he give him a stone? or if he ask a fish will he for a fish give him a serpent? or if he shall ask an egg, will he offer him a scorpion? Yet ye being evil know how to give good gifts unto your children, how much more shall your heavenly father give the holy spirit to them that ask him."

After reading this I would say: "O my Father in heaven, I am a father; I have children, I love them as I love my own soul; my children never asked of me a fish and got a serpent; they never asked an egg and got turned away with a scorpion. O, thou who lovest me more than I love my children; thou who hast said, "Yea, a mother may forget the child she bear, but I cannot forget thee; thou who lovest me more than a mother ever loved her child, I pray thee, give me thy holy spirit."

And in answer to that prayer, more than ten thousand times repeated, Spiritualism came to me.

Now, do you tell me that God has insulted my most honest and earnest prayer by uncapping hell and letting legions of damned devils loose upon me? Is that your God? If so, it is well to serve the devil. No devil could do so devilish a trick as that. I do not love a God who would do that. I could not. I could not allow my lips to tell the lie they would utter in saying I love him.

Nay, let me go one step farther; if there is a devil please tell me who made him? Did God make him? Was it not a devilish trick for God to make a devil and turn him loose on his innocent children? Do you say God did not make him, that he exists contrary to the power of God? Then God is not

God; something exists which he did not make and cannot control! (In one case God is wicked, in the other he is weak.)

I will ask one more question: Why does not God kill the devil? or at least take his power for evil away from him? If God had my goodness, or if I had his power, the sting would be taken away from this devil; his power for mischief would be annihilated ere the setting of another sun.

When I ask this question, I am answered, "God will kill him." I answer, That does not suit me. Why did he not exterminate him six thousand years ago? Six thousand years is a long time to allow this arch fiend his power for evil.

If I had the power to kill the snake or the tarantula which is striving every moment to kill your children, would it satisfy you for me to say, I will kill him; I simply want to wait and see what mischief he can do. No, it would not, nor am I satisfied with a God who gives the devil such loose rein for so many thousand years.

No; the devil does not exist. The lamented William Denton satirizes the matter as follows:

Sigh, priests; cry aloud, hang your pulpits with
    black;
  Let sorrow bow down every head;
The good friend who bore all your sins on his back,
  Your best friend, the Devil, is dead.

Your church is a corpse; you are guarding its
    tomb;
  The soul of your system has fled.
That death-knell is tolling your terrible doom;
  It tells us the Devil is dead.

'Twas knowledge gave Satan a terrible blow;
  Poor fellow! he took to his bed.
Alas! idle priests, that such things should be so;
  Your master, the Devil, is dead.

You're bid to the funeral, ministers all;
  We've dug the old gentleman's bed;
Your black coats will make a most excellent pall
  To cover your friend who is dead.

Ay, lower him mournfully into the grave;
  Let showers of tear-drops be shed;
Your business is gone; there are no souls to save;
  Their tempter, the Devil, is dead.

Woe comes upon woe; you can ne'er get your dues.
  Hell's open; the damned souls have fled;
They took to their heels when they heard the good
    news,—
  Their jailer, the Devil, is dead.

Camp-meetings henceforth will be needed no more;
  Revivals are knocked on the head;
The orthodox vessel lies stranded on shore,
  Her captain, the Devil, is dead.

Teaching Materials included

Scan this code to get
your Video Course included in the book, an introduction to the world of the occult and the paranormal

Or follow this link:

https://templumdianae.co/the-witchy-course/

This Material will give you access to Exclusive training materials to improve in your path !

All rights reserved. No part of this book may be reproduced in any form without the written permission of the copyright owners. All images in this book have been reproduced with the knowledge and prior consent of the artists concerned, and the producer, publisher, or printer accepts no responsibility for any infringement of copyright or otherwise, arising from the contents of this publication. Every effort has been made to ensure that the credits accurately conform to the information provided. We apologize for any inaccuracies and will correct inaccurate or missing information in a subsequent reprint of the book.

Text © 2023 Templum Dianae Media